INTRODUCTION

Entropia, also known as chaos, is a term that describes the degree of randomness or disorder in a system. It is a known fact that all things within the universe prefer to exist in a state of chaos because it requires less energy to do so. I am a scientist by training, so when I formed Entropia Consulting in 2009, my goal was to be a source of energy that brought order to the chaos that my clients were experiencing.

Leaders, whether leading an organization, a team, or self, need to be challenged, inspired and motivated. I often use short, thought-provoking phrases as sources of energy to help people become the best leader they can be. This book is a collection of some of my favorite sayings.

As you read through the quotes and one resonates with you, or speaks to something you are experiencing, spend some time reflecting on it. Then, write an actionable item that you will commit to doing that addresses it. Whether you choose to read these daily, weekly or monthly, I encourage you to use them as quick energy bites whenever you need to bring order to the chaos in your leadership!

Interested in making Entropia a part of your success? Dr. Qualls is available for consulting, coaching, or speaking engagements. For more information and booking, contact her at
entropia@entropiaconsulting.com
or visit her website at entropiaconsulting.com.

Copyright (c) 2018 by Entropia Consulting
ISBN: 9781718103191

They That Wait...
Isaiah 40:31

We are the sum of the people and experiences that we encounter along our life's journey. I am grateful and appreciative of my family, friends and colleagues who have supported me as I pursue my passion. Things have not always gone smoothly nor orderly...but if it did, there would be no Entropia!

Talent alone is not enough, because the world is full of talent. You've got to be willing to take risks and go the extra miles to attain your success.

Reflections and Actions

Reflections and Actions

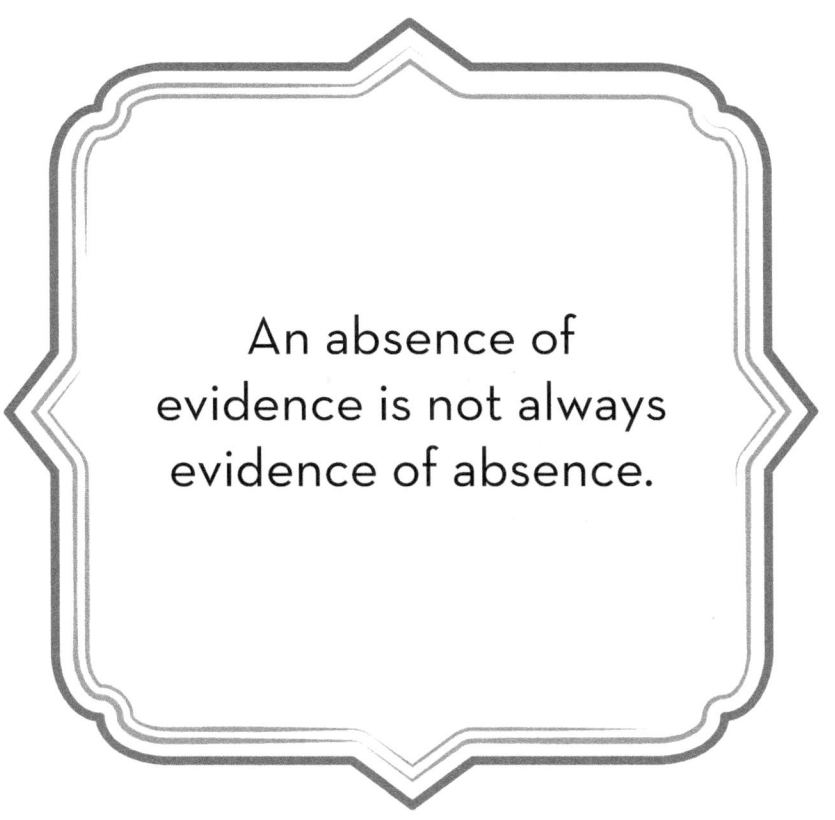

An absence of evidence is not always evidence of absence.

A common trait among successful people is a will to win, and more importantly, a will to PREPARE to win.

Reflections and Actions

Reflections and Actions

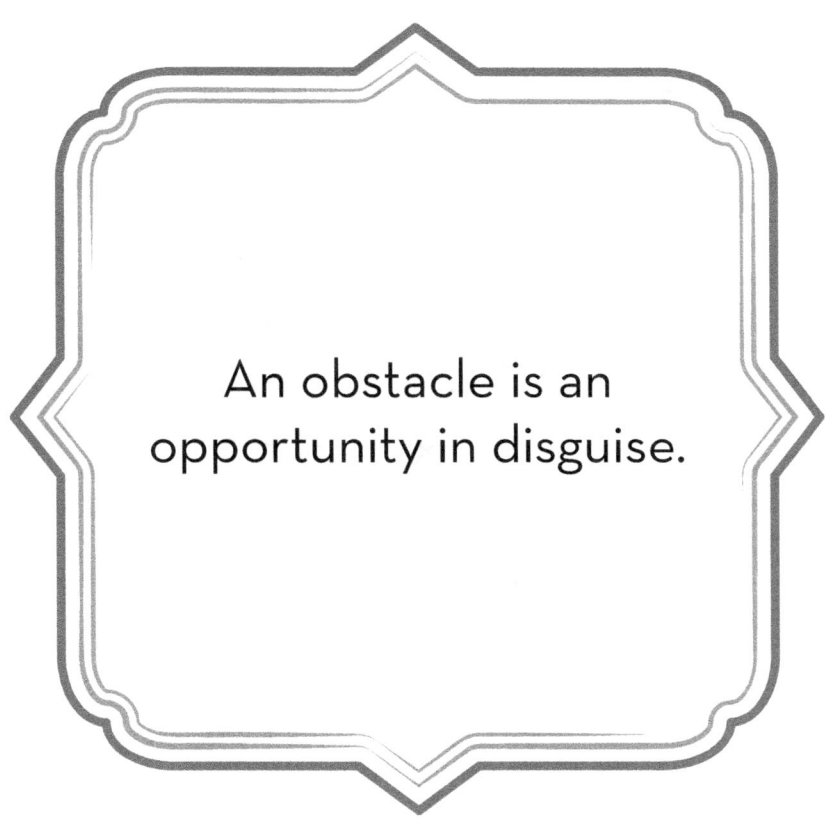

An obstacle is an opportunity in disguise.

Always thank the person who gives you feedback — even if it is negative. It may shine light on a blind spot that's hindering you from being your best.

Reflections and Actions

Reflections and Actions

Are you willing to be a follower? Are you capable of being led?

Be comfortable with who you are and confident in your abilities. There is at least one thing that you do better than anyone else, and that's what makes you unique!

Reflections and Actions

Reflections and Actions

Asking others for help shows strength. Allowing others to help shows confidence. Helping others shows growth.

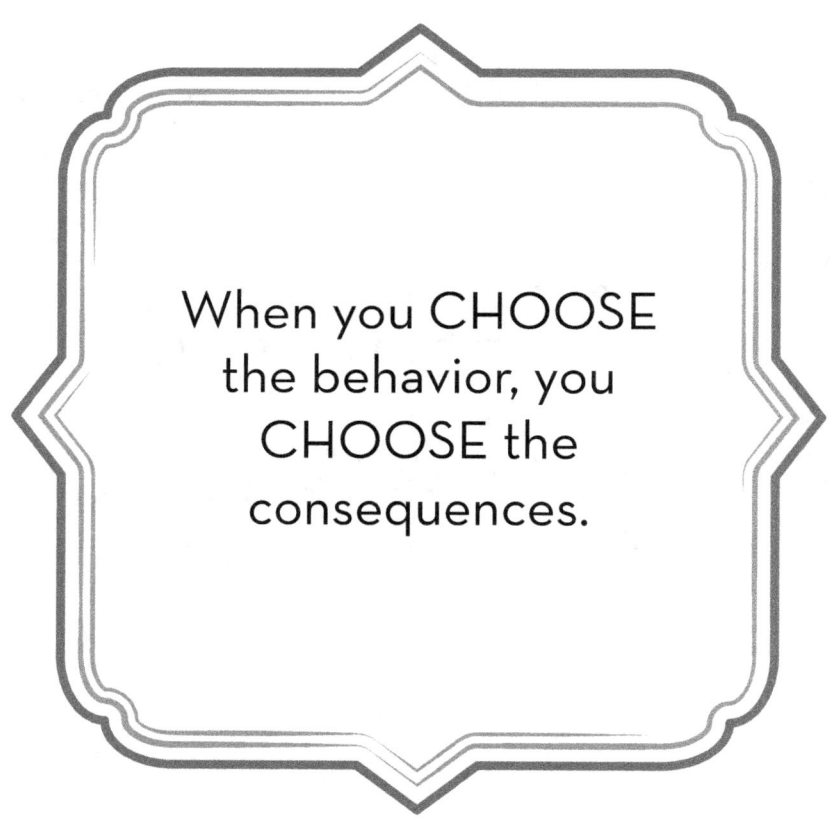

When you CHOOSE the behavior, you CHOOSE the consequences.

Reflections and Actions

Reflections and Actions

Be realistic with your expectations.

If you never say NO,
what does your YES
really mean?

Reflections and Actions

Reflections and Actions

Delayed just means it will happen later than what's on YOUR timetable.

Busy leads to Burnout. Learn to master the skill of leverage by using your time, knowledge and resources to create win-win situations that free up space and allow you to be more productive and less busy.

Reflections and Actions

Reflections and Actions

Be careful of who you allow to represent you and tell your story.

Doing the same things and expecting different results may be the definition of insanity, but it may also be a sign of denial and stubbornness.

Reflections and Actions

Reflections and Actions

Don't change who you are because of where you are.

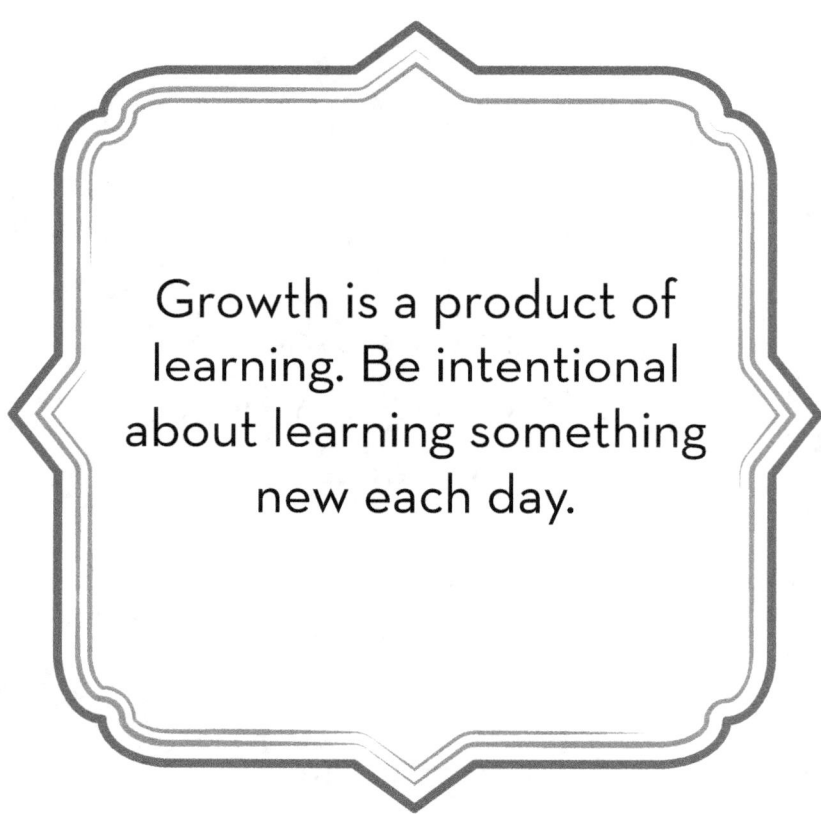

Growth is a product of learning. Be intentional about learning something new each day.

Reflections and Actions

Reflections and Actions

Endings can lead to great beginnings.

Golden is the spot that captures your purpose, passion, experiences and strengths.

Reflections and Actions

Reflections and Actions

Growth and Comfort rarely co-exist.

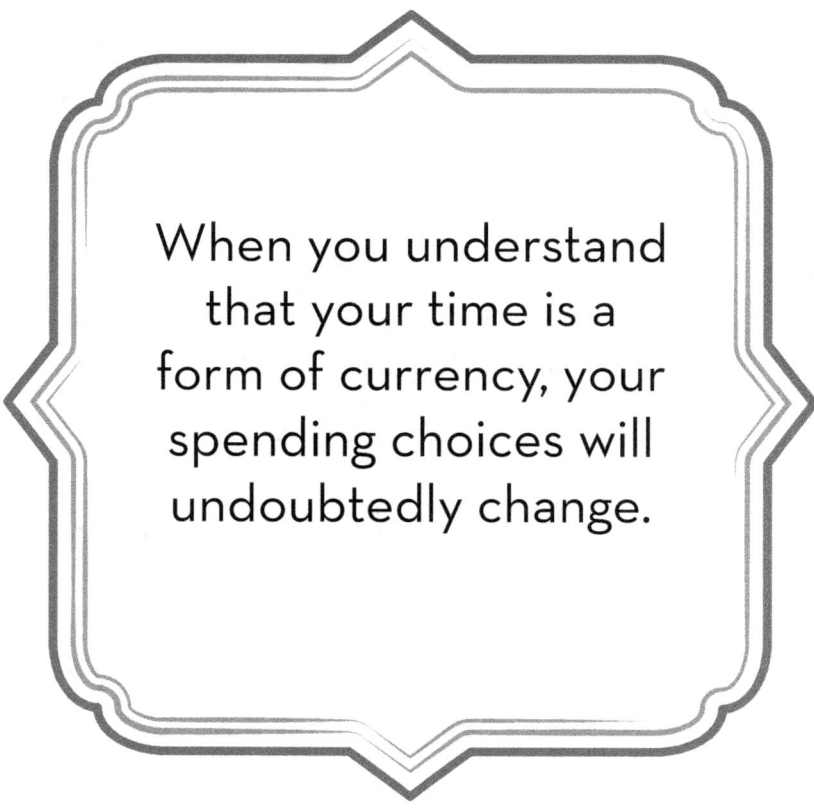

When you understand that your time is a form of currency, your spending choices will undoubtedly change.

Reflections and Actions

Reflections and Actions

Growth is being able to celebrate small successes and big failures.

Encourage someone today in their endeavors. Your simple words or small act of support may be that extra push they need to have a major breakthrough.

Reflections and Actions

Reflections and Actions

Every conversation does not require a solution.

If it is something that you really want, a 'NO' will not deter you. You will FIND A WAY to get it done.

Reflections and Actions

Reflections and Actions

How often do you reflect, refocus, and re-prioritize?

If you aren't willing to invest in yourself, why do you expect anyone else to do so?

Reflections and Actions

Reflections and Actions

Improvement begins from within.

If you want to grow, you have to venture and operate outside of your comfort zone.

Reflections and Actions

Reflections and Actions

Never underestimate the power of a question.

It won't always be a straight path that leads you to your destination. There may be several twists, turns, and bumps along the way, but it's important to KEEP GOING FORWARD despite any obstacles or crooked paths you encounter.

Reflections and Actions

Reflections and Actions

Know Your Value.
Know Your Worth.

In your quest to do better and be better, answer these two simple questions: What will you continue to do? What will you do differently?

Reflections and Actions

Reflections and Actions

Learn to use collaboration for a competitive advantage.

Learning to deal with difficult people is a valuable and necessary skill--especially when that person is the one you see in the mirror.

Reflections and Actions

Reflections and Actions

Letting other people lead shows the leader in you.

It's easy to be grateful for what you have. However, it is equally important to be thankful for those things that you don't have.

Reflections and Actions

Reflections and Actions

Live intentionally! Life is a journey to be explored and enjoyed.

Making a career or life change is similar to eating. We know we need to do it, but too often we wait until the hunger pains are unbearable and we are physically, mentally, and emotionally weak before we take action.

Reflections and Actions

Reflections and Actions

Say what you mean, and mean what you say.

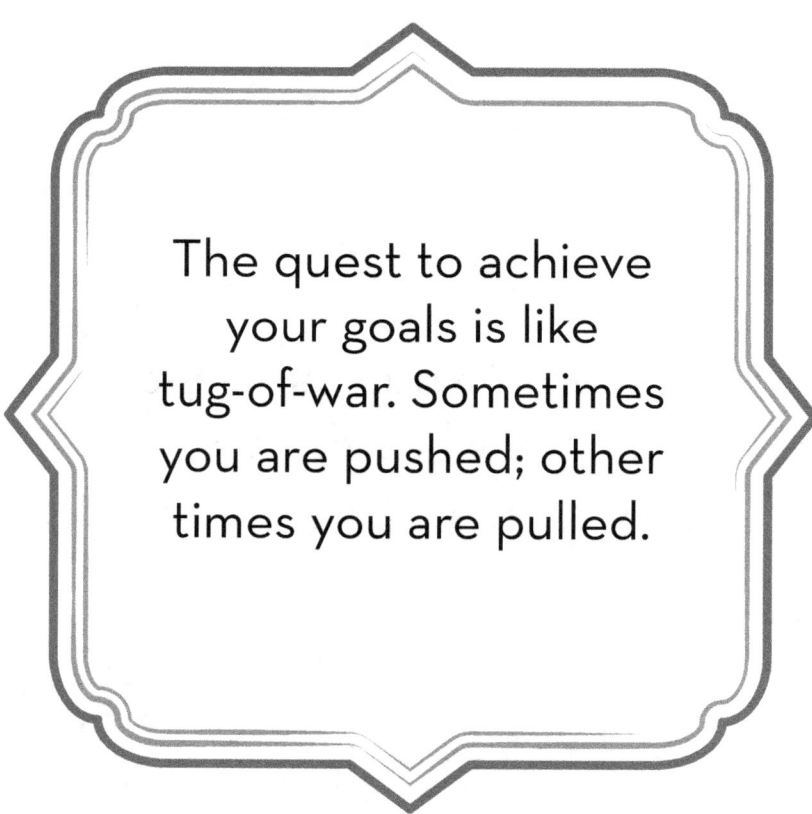

The quest to achieve your goals is like tug-of-war. Sometimes you are pushed; other times you are pulled.

Reflections and Actions

Reflections and Actions

Sometimes it takes 100 NO responses to PREPARE you for that 1 YES.

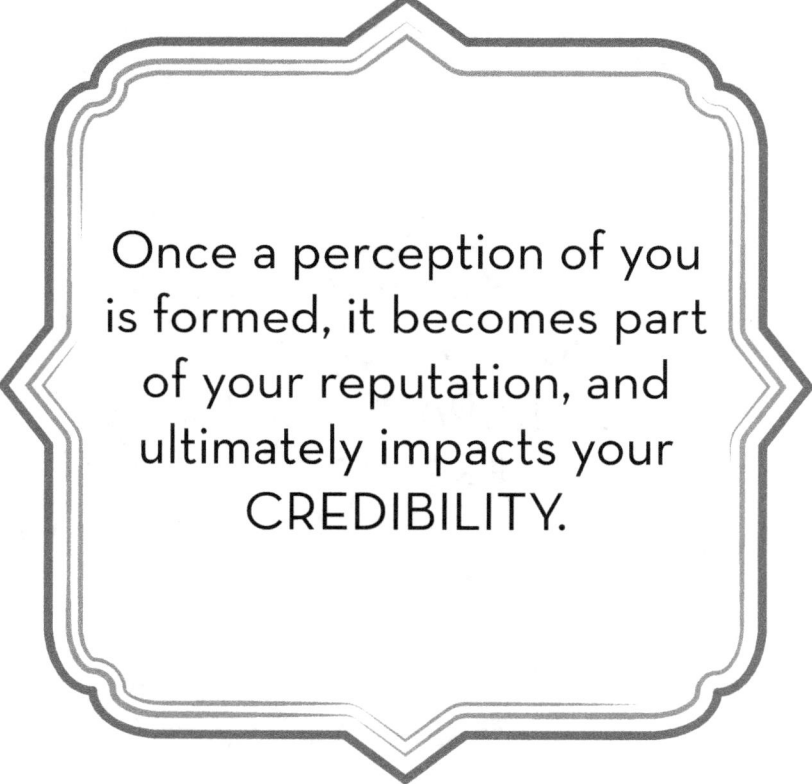

Once a perception of you is formed, it becomes part of your reputation, and ultimately impacts your CREDIBILITY.

Reflections and Actions

Reflections and Actions

Sometimes even when you get it right, you get it wrong.

Sacrifice, Determination, Discipline, Dedication: The things you do [and don't do] today should be the things that prepare you for where you want to be tomorrow.

Reflections and Actions

Reflections and Actions

Start doing the things that feed your passion!

Seek advice from those who have experience in resolving conflict rather than doing it your way and making matters worse.

Reflections and Actions

Reflections and Actions

Today is THE day that I will...

The path of least resistance may be the easier option, but your growth happens when you persevere through the challenges and obstacles of the less traveled road. Things may not get easier, but you will be better equipped to handle whatever comes your way in the future.

Reflections and Actions

Reflections and Actions

We all have a light in us. Don't be afraid to let it shine.

Time is the currency for every activity you engage. Talk is cheap, which explains why most people would rather spend their time talking about it than being about it.

Reflections and Actions

Reflections and Actions

When you expand your circle, you become exposed to a whole new world.

Silence is not the absence of a message, but IS a message. Listen to what people are saying to you.

Reflections and Actions

Reflections and Actions

Multitasking is counterproductive and divides your focus.

You have to do your own growing no matter how tall your parents are.

Reflections and Actions

Reflections and Actions

Know when to let go.
There is a sunset behind
every storm.

Be proactive. Don't wait for a crisis to happen and you are forced to get things in order.

Reflections and Actions

Reflections and Actions

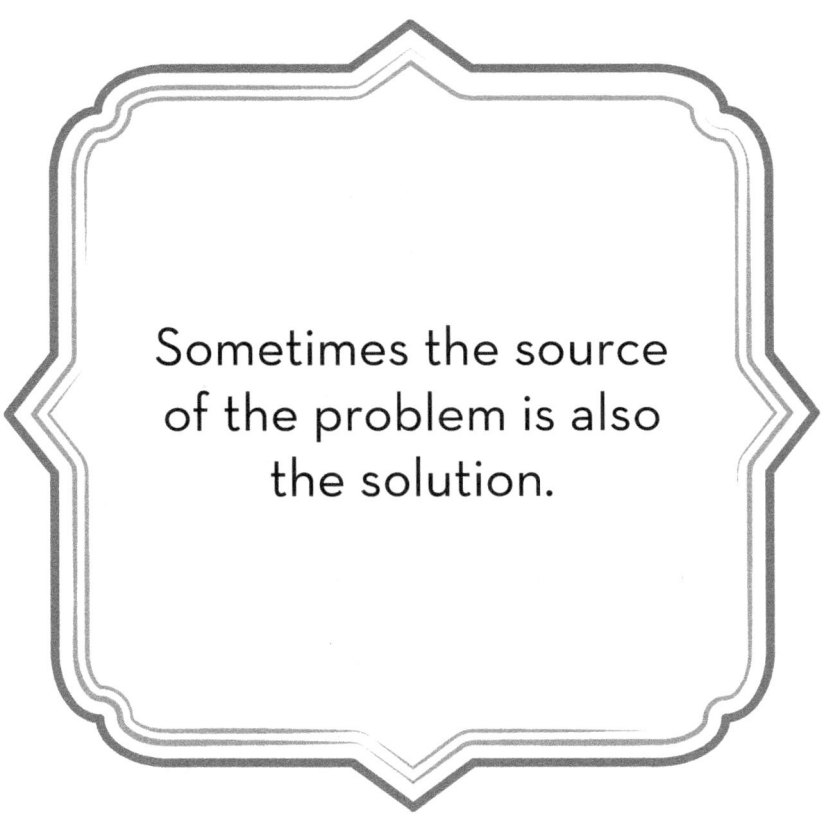

Sometimes the source of the problem is also the solution.

Too often we strive for perfection when it is through mistakes that we learn the greatest lessons and experience the most growth. Be courageous enough today to make a mistake.

Reflections and Actions

Reflections and Actions

You can only do what YOU can do.

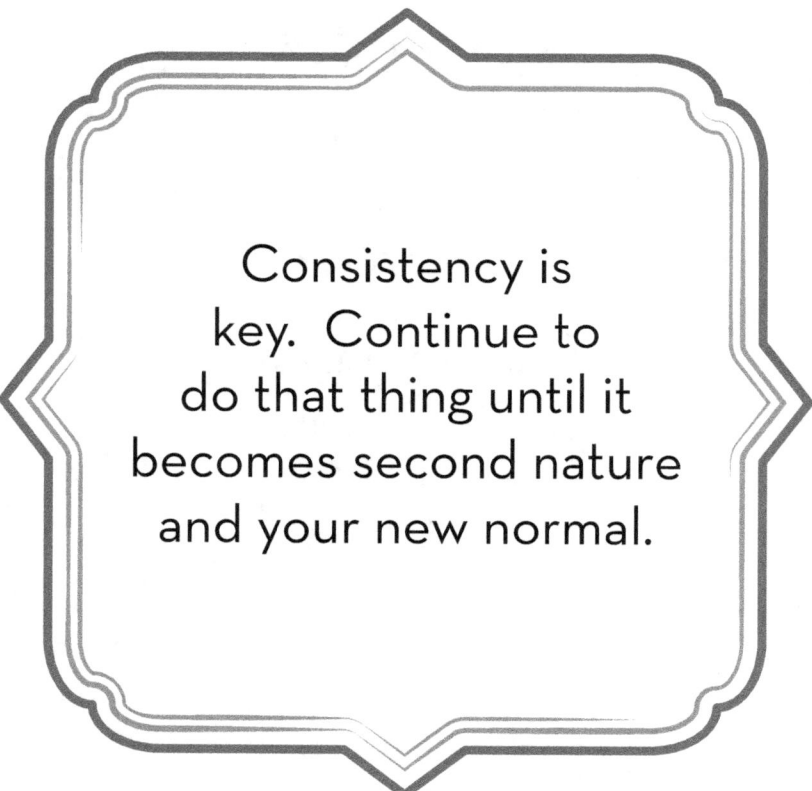

Consistency is key. Continue to do that thing until it becomes second nature and your new normal.

Reflections and Actions

Reflections and Actions

Today may not be perfect, but it does have PURPOSE!

Appreciate the detours, roadblocks and U-Turns that occur in your personal and professional life. They are for your protection.

Reflections and Actions

Reflections and Actions

It's not over, until you are done.

Wanting it is not enough. You must be willing to commit and make the necessary investment [time and/or money] to do what it takes to get it.

Reflections and Actions

Reflections and Actions

Rest and Relaxation are essential for success.

Time is the currency for every activity you engage. Talk is cheap, which explains why most people would rather spend their time talking about it than being about it.

Reflections and Actions

Reflections and Actions

If you don't have time to do it right, when will you have time to do it over?

When you understand the CONTEXT, the CONTENT is easier to digest.

Reflections and Actions

Reflections and Actions

The thing you are holding back is the thing holding you back.

Don't dismiss sage advice because you think the person has not lived enough years. Wisdom comes from experience, not just age.

Reflections and Actions

Reflections and Actions

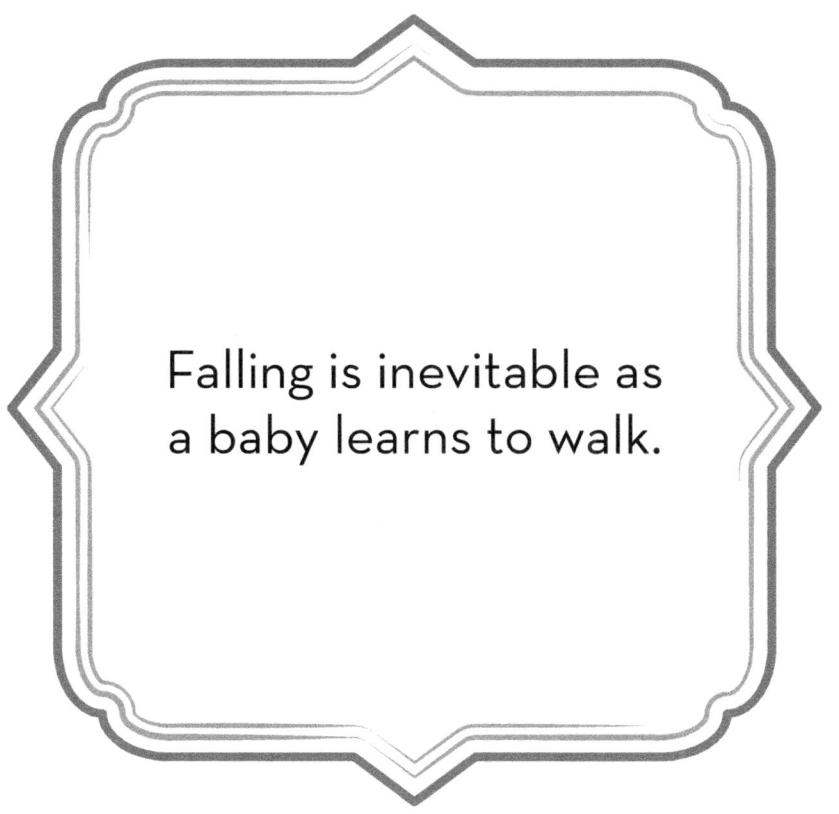

Falling is inevitable as a baby learns to walk.

You are your greatest asset. When you show a commitment and willingness to invest in yourself, others are more likely to assist you in achieving your goals.

Reflections and Actions

Reflections and Actions

True independence comes when you are comfortable and confident in asking for assistance.

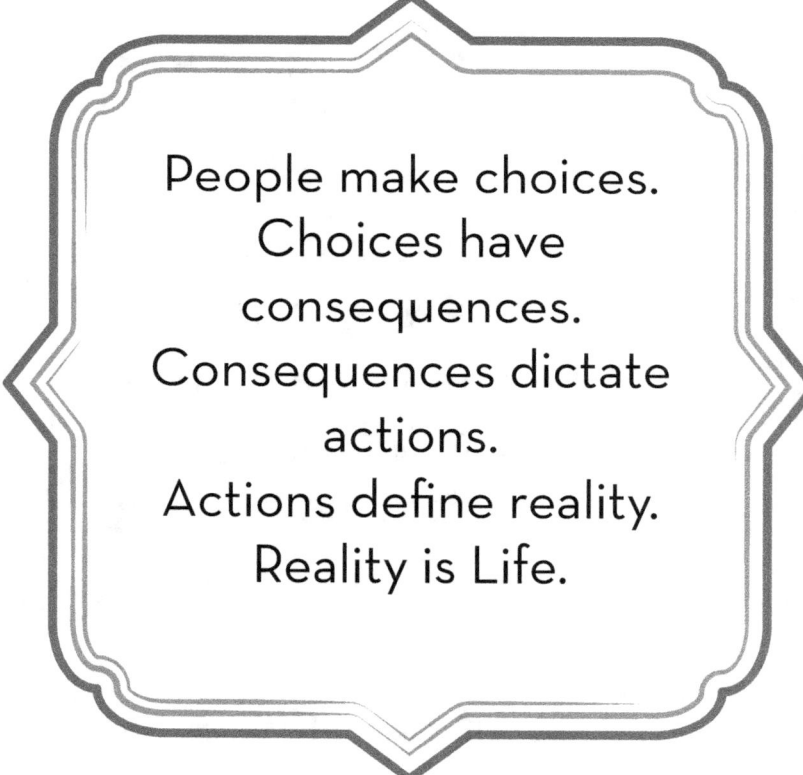

People make choices.
Choices have consequences.
Consequences dictate actions.
Actions define reality.
Reality is Life.

Reflections and Actions

Reflections and Actions

Your standard of excellence dictates the people in your presence.

Don't confuse the people who are always around with the ones who are always there.

Reflections and Actions

Reflections and Actions

Clarity allows you to be less frustrated with your situation, and less frustrating to those around you.

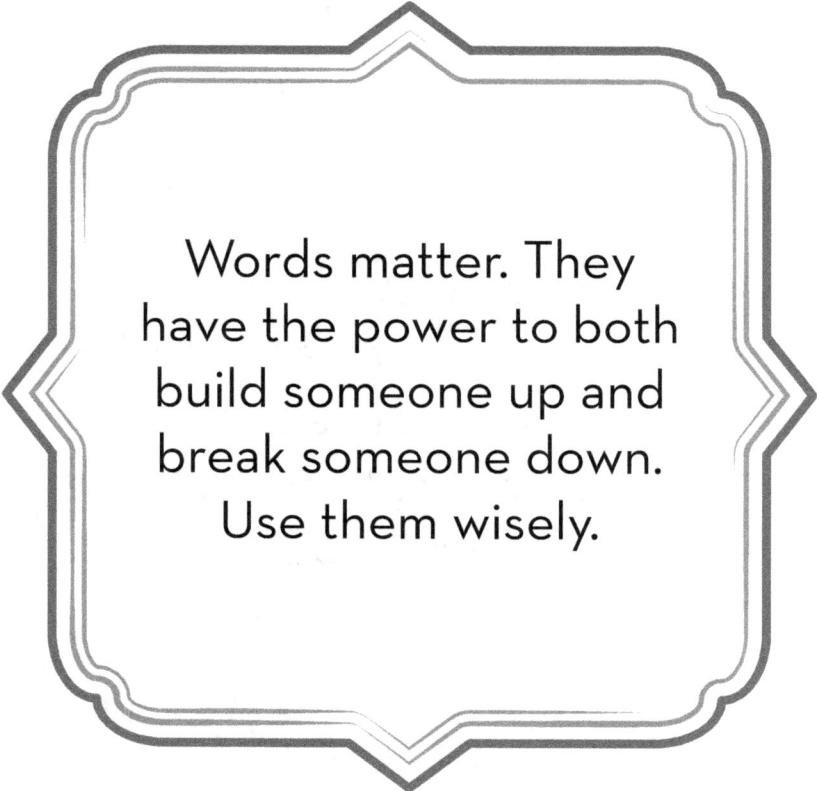

Words matter. They have the power to both build someone up and break someone down. Use them wisely.

Reflections and Actions

Reflections and Actions

When you are invited to sit at the table...EAT and PARTAKE in the discussion!

When you are willing to admit what you don't know, and are open to trying something new, true learning and growth occurs.

Reflections and Actions

Reflections and Actions

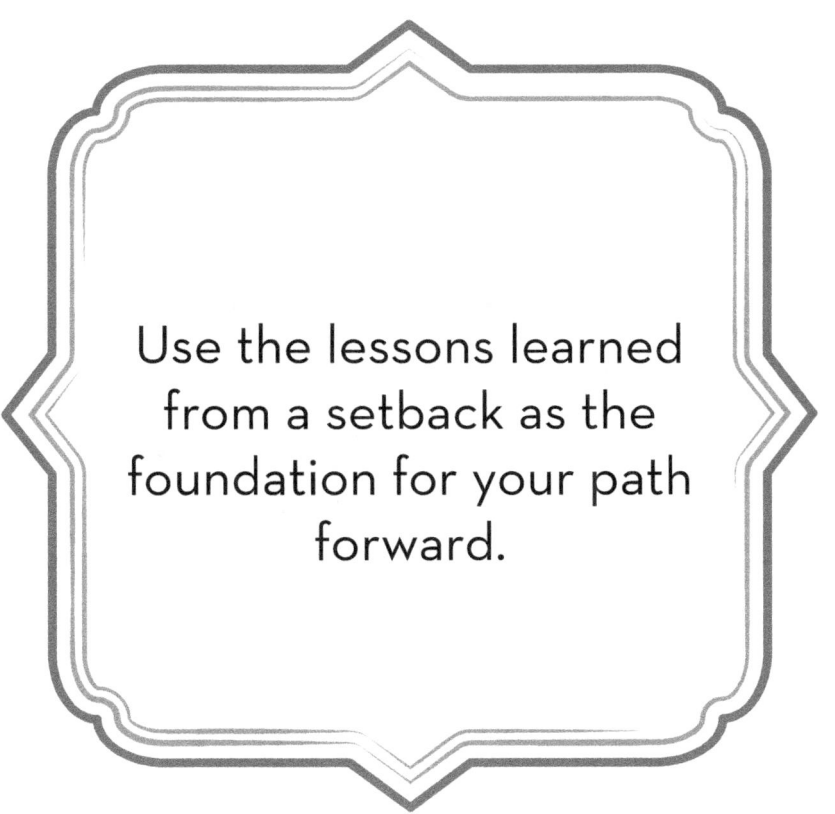

Use the lessons learned from a setback as the foundation for your path forward.

When you find yourself contributing instead of growing, it is time for a change.

Reflections and Actions

Reflections and Actions

Your personal brand should represent your commitment to quality and excellence.

ASAP stands for : As Soon As Possible. That does not mean Drop Everything and Do it NOW.

Reflections and Actions

Reflections and Actions

Define or be defined.

Even though you may get a second chance, always remember that first impressions are lasting.

Reflections and Actions

Reflections and Actions

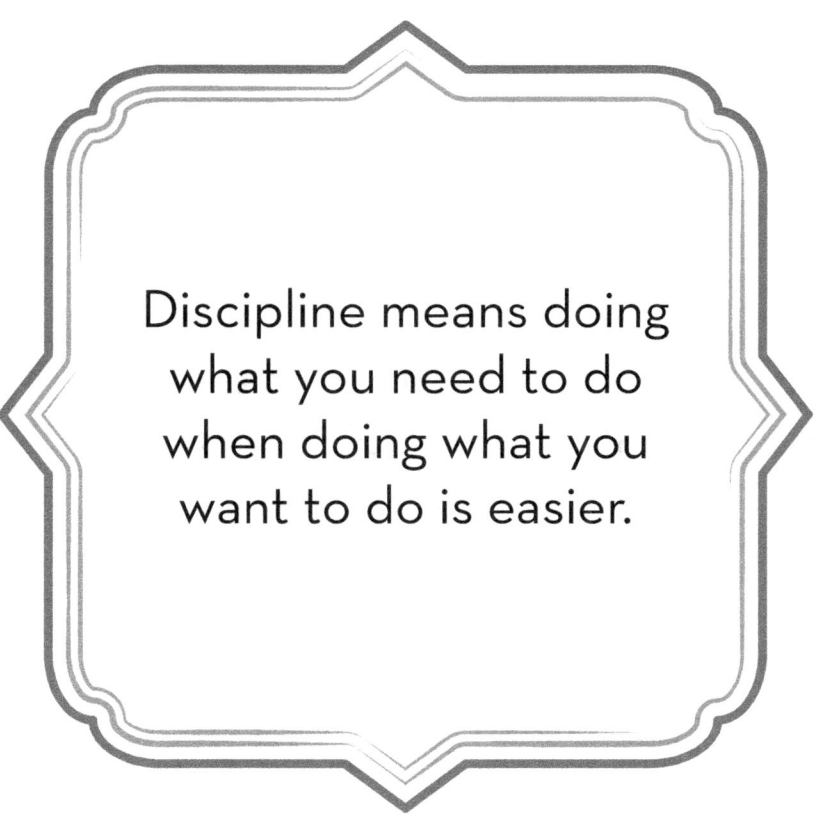

Discipline means doing what you need to do when doing what you want to do is easier.

Now that you know better, how will you do better?

Reflections and Actions

Marquita M. Qualls, PhD, also known as 'Dr. Q', has over 25 years of leadership experience in consulting, coaching, and motivating to produce order out of the chaos (entropia!). A scientist by training, her style is often described as energetic, engaging, and empowering. She possesses the rare combination of strong technical ability and impressive soft skills, which enables her to function and make seamless transitions between the scientific and non-technical worlds. Her technical side drives an ability to gather perspectives and analyze feedback, while at the same time connecting with clients and guiding them towards achieving results.

www.ingramcontent.com/pod-product-compliance
Lightning Source LLC
Chambersburg PA
CBHW052316220526
45472CB00001B/141